SCIENCE ON ICE

Science on Ice

RESEARCH IN THE ANTARCTIC

MICHAEL WOODS

THE MILLBROOK PRESS
BROOKFIELD, CONNECTICUT

Cover photograph courtesy of Superstock

Photographs courtesy of the National Science Foundation
except pp. 8, 10, 27, 75, 78: Michael Woods; p. 13: Bettmann;
NASA: p. 37. Map by Frank Senyk.

Library of Congress Cataloging-in-Publication Data

Woods, Michael, 1946–
Science on ice : research in the Antarctic / by Michael Woods.
p.   cm.
Includes bibliographical references and index.
Summary: surveys scientific work being done in the Antarctic
and its local as well as global applications.
ISBN 1-56294-498-3 (lib. bdg.)
1. Antarctica—Juvenile literature.   [1. Antarctica.]   I. Title.
G863.W66   1995   919.8'9—dc20   94-12055   CIP   AC

Published by The Millbrook Press, Inc.
2 Old New Milford Road, Brookfield, Connecticut 06804

Librarians play an important role in introducing young people to books that reveal the wonders of science. Interest awakened by a book sometimes grows and blossoms into a career. Librarians and their books hooked many of us on a life in science. One school librarian, my wife, Mary Woods, inspired me to help by writing this book. Four young people—our children Jeremy, Matthew, Cathleen, and Margaret—acted as critics. This book is dedicated to them, with thanks for their advice during the writing and patience during the long absences while I worked on the frozen continent.

CONTENTS

1

A CONTINENT
FOR SCIENCE

The temperature soars to minus 42 degrees Fahrenheit (−41°C) on this warm spring afternoon, as I stand at the very bottom of the world, Antarctica. Here, the cold gets so intense that it can shatter a person's teeth and instantly freeze exposed skin. Today's temperature of −42°F *really is* warm.

Clutches of scientists have emerged from the warmth of America's Amundsen-Scott South Pole Station, nestled beneath a huge aluminum dome a few minutes walk from the geographic South Pole. The station is named for Roald Amundsen and Robert Falcon Scott, figures from the Age of Heroes, the first and most familiar era of antarctic exploration. These first explorers came for adventure, but sometimes they found terrible suffering and death in Earth's most hostile environment. Amundsen was the Norwegian explorer who, on December 14, 1911, won a dramatic, worldwide race to become the first person to reach the South Pole. Fewer than 30,000 people have stood here since. Scott, a British explorer, arrived thirty-five days later to find a Norwegian flag planted at the pole, and a message from the triumphant Amundsen. Disappointed, exhausted, starving, Scott and the four members of his expedition died trying to get back.

Across the vast polar plateau, against a horizon of white ice and azure blue sky, I watch the scientists. On foot and in big, tracked vehicles called Sno-Cats, they head for nearby huts and

A Sno-Cat carries scientists to research huts at the South Pole.

shelters crammed with scientific instruments. There they will study problems as remote as the origin of the universe 15 billion years ago, and as immediate as depletion of Earth's protective ozone layer.

They are figures from the new age of antarctic exploration, the Age of Science.

I accompanied these men and women, these new explorers, during three research seasons in 1991, 1993, and 1994 from one end of the Antarctic to another, as they studied subjects ranging from astronomy to zoology. They were Americans, Russians, Chinese, Chileans—people from thirteen countries that maintain bases and conduct scientific research in the Antarctic. They worked in isolated huts and tents; with scuba gear in 28°F (−2°C) water under ice 5 feet (1.5 meters) thick; on islands carpeted with thousands of nesting penguins; on tiny, inflatable raftlike Zodiacs; and on research vessels longer than a football field that could crunch through ice 18 feet (5.5 meters) thick.

Many early antarctic expeditions did include meteorologists, geologists, and other scientists. But science was only one reason for coming to Earth's most isolated place. Now it is emerging as the main reason. The Antarctic is being transformed into a continent for science, the world's biggest research facility, a living laboratory larger than the United States and Mexico combined. It is the only continent reserved by treaty for scientific research. With the Antarctic's transformation has come a new sense of stewardship, in which scientists and visitors take great care to avoid damaging the environment.

THE CONTINENT OPPOSITE THE BEAR

Antarctica was a legend long before its reality became known. Ancient Greek philosophers believed that a perfect symmetry, or balance, occurred in nature, and speculated that a southern landmass must exist to balance the northern landmasses. They gave that supposed landmass the name Antarctica, which comes from Greek words meaning "opposite the bear." The "bear" is Ursa Major, a constellation visible in the Northern Hemisphere. In the sixteenth and seventeenth centuries, explorers from Spain, Portugal, and other countries searched for the continent, which had become known as *Terra Australis*, Southern Land. Legend told of a paradise strewn with nuggets of gold and other treasures. Early in the nineteenth century, people thought there was an entrance to the interior of Earth at the South Pole. According to some accounts, the U.S. Congress even considered sending a military expedition to find the South Pole, go inside Earth, and make contact with people living there.

The first reported sighting of the antarctic continent occurred in 1820, a time when sailing ships hunted whales and seals in the region. Historians disagree on who discovered Antarctica. But many believe that in 1820 three men, on separate occasions, spotted the Antarctic Peninsula, a finger of land that points out from western Antarctica toward South America. They were an American, Nathaniel B. Palmer; a Russian, Fabian von Bellingshausen; and Britain's Edward Bransfield. The first American scientist soon visited the Antarctic. He was James Eights, a geologist from Albany, New York. In 1830 he studied land features in the South Shetland Islands and along the Antarctic Peninsula. Charles Wilkes, a U. S. Navy lieutenant, confirmed the existence of the antarctic continent on mapping expeditions in 1839 and 1840.

EARLY EXPEDITIONS

During the rest of the 1800s and early 1900s, several countries dispatched exploring and mapping expeditions to Antarctica. After arctic explorers reached the North Pole in 1909, the race to the South Pole captured the excitement of people around the world. In 1911, expeditions from five countries—Norway, Britain, Germany, Australia, and Japan—were competing for the honor of being first to reach the South Pole.

One of the most famous episodes in the Antarctic's Age of Heroes began in 1914, when British explorer Ernest Shackleton set out on a bold effort to cross the antarctic continent by dog sledge. The ship *Endurance*, which carried Shackleton and his expedition to the Antarctic, was beset—frozen—in the treacherous Weddell Sea. Rescue was out of the question. They were 1,200 miles (1,931 kilometers) from the nearest inhabited land. There was no radio to summon help and no helicopters to bring it; nobody in the outside world even knew their whereabouts. For months the ice squeezed in on the ship. Finally, the pressure crushed and sank the *Endurance*. The crew

British explorer Robert Falcon Scott (standing, center) and his expedition reached the South Pole in January 1912—only to find that the Norwegian Roald Amundsen had arrived weeks earlier. Scott and his four companions died on the way back.

escaped to an ice floe, a sheet of floating ice, with two small wooden boats, sledges, dogs, and supplies. There they drifted for months, as the terrible antarctic winter closed in. Winter in the Antarctic can mean not just temperatures that may plummet below −100°F (−73°C), and winds that exceed 100 miles per hour (160 kph), but six months of darkness and absolute isolation. Housed in flimsy tents, with temperatures as low as −35°F (−37°C), dressed in primitive cold-weather clothing, Shackleton's expedition survived by eating dog food, penguins, seal blubber, and, according to some, even their own precious sled dogs.

(13)

They finally were rescued in 1916, after a team led by Shackleton completed one of the most amazing feats in the history of exploration. They sailed a small boat through 870 miles (1,400 kilometers) of some of the roughest seas on Earth to get help at a whaling station. Amazingly, all of the men survived.

Although these tales of adventure thrilled the world, United States interest in the Antarctic lay dormant until 1928, when U. S. Navy Commander Richard E. Byrd led the first of two privately sponsored antarctic expeditions. Byrd established an American base, Little America I, close to Roald Amundsen's old base in the Bay of Whales. In 1929, Byrd amazed the world by flying over the South Pole in a Ford Trimotor airplane. He took photographs critical for mapping parts of the antarctic interior, which truly was *terra incognita*, an unexplored region. The feat led to many additional aerial mapping flights. For instance, aerial photography was used extensively during Operation High Jump. This big American effort to explore the Antarctic, conducted in 1946–1947, involved thirteen ships, many airplanes and helicopters, and more than 4,700 men who collected masses of data about antarctic geography and meteorology.

THE WORLD'S COLDEST LABORATORY

The modern era of antarctic exploration opened with the International Geophysical Year (IGY) of 1957–1958. The IGY was the biggest scientific research program ever conducted in the Antarctic, a worldwide cooperative effort involving scientists from twelve nations at over fifty different research stations. America set up six research stations, including one at the geographic South Pole. The Soviet Union's stations included one at the Pole of Inaccessibility, the site on the antarctic continent most distant from all the coasts. Researchers studied gravitational and magnetic fields; measured the depth of polar ice sheets; took readings of ocean temperature, depth, and circulation patterns; and continued efforts to map the continent's geographical features.

The IGY led to the first broad understanding of the physical factors that shape the Antarctic. But most important, the findings led the United States and other nations to establish permanent bases for conducting antarctic research on a continuing basis. The twelve nations that participated in the IGY negotiated an agreement to use the Antarctic for scientific research and other peaceful purposes. It prohibited military activities, nuclear explosions, and disposal of nuclear waste, and encouraged international cooperation on scientific research. The nations signed the agreement, called the Antarctic Treaty, in 1959.

Since then, an additional twenty-nine nations have agreed to honor the treaty's provisions. The Antarctic Treaty nations represent about two thirds of Earth's population. Meetings are held every two years to discuss other measures needed to maintain the Antarctic as a continent for science. In 1991, participants signed an agreement to ban mining and take additional steps to protect the environment.

Since 1959, the National Science Foundation (NSF) has had responsibility for America's ongoing scientific research program in the Antarctic. (NSF is an independent agency of the federal government that funds many different kinds of scientific research at colleges, universities, and other facilities.) Called the U. S. Antarctic Research Program, it involves more than 120 different projects in areas of science such as astronomy, biology, climatology, oceanography, geology, and glaciology. Through the 1980s and early 1990s, NSF spent about $200 million each year on the Antarctic Research Program. During that time, about 2,500 Americans worked in and around Antarctica as part of the program each year. They included scientists from many universities who conducted research, as well as support personnel who operated airplanes, helicopters, research stations, and other facilities.

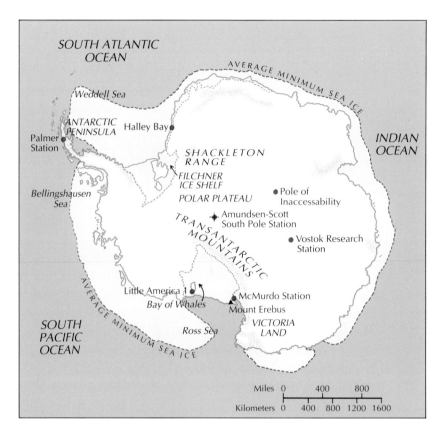

SOUTH ATLANTIC
OCEAN

AVERAGE MINIMUM SEA ICE

Weddell Sea

ANTARCTIC
PENINSULA   Halley Bay

Palmer
Station

INDIAN
OCEAN

SHACKLETON
RANGE

FILCHNER
ICE SHELF

Bellingshausen
Sea

POLAR PLATEAU

Pole of
Inaccessability

TRANSANTARCTIC
MOUNTAINS

Amundsen-Scott
South Pole Station

Vostok Research
Station

AVERAGE MINIMUM SEA ICE

Little America 1

Bay of Whales

McMurdo Station

Mount Erebus

SOUTH
PACIFIC
OCEAN

Ross Sea

VICTORIA
LAND

Miles   0   400   800

Kilometers 0   400   800 1200 1600

Facts on Antarctica

CLIMATE: Antarctica is the coldest, windiest, driest, highest, most inhospitable continent on Earth. The world's record low temperature, minus 128.6 degrees Fahrenheit (−89.2°C), was recorded there in 1983 at Russia's Vostok research station deep in the continent's interior.[3] Refrigerators for fresh foods and soft drinks at America's Amundsen-Scott South Pole Station are *heated*. Wind gusts of 199 miles per hour (320 kph) have been recorded. Except for rain and drizzle in the

Antarctic Peninsula, precipitation is almost entirely snow. But Antarctica gets so little precipitation that it is the world's biggest and driest desert. Interior areas, for instance, get the equivalent of only 1 to 2 inches (2.5 to 5 centimeters) of rainfall each year. Central Antarctica has six months of winter darkness and six months of summer when the sun never sets. The seasons are reversed; with summer in the Northern Hemisphere being winter in Antarctica.

LAND FEATURES: Antarctica has an area of 5.4 million square miles (almost 14 million square kilometers).[4] Snow and ice cover 98 percent of the continent.[5] The only visible land is mountain peaks and rock-strewn areas called dry valleys. Glaciers or ice caps cover 5.3 million square miles, and are up to 3 miles (4.8 kilometers) thick. If the ice were melted, it would raise global ocean levels by 200 feet (60.9 meters)[6]. The ice makes Antarctica the world's highest continent in terms of average elevation, which is 7,100 feet (2,164 meters) above sea level. As glaciers flow to the coast, big chunks break off and fall into the sea as icebergs. Enough ice reaches the sea this way every year to supply 65 percent of the world's freshwater consumption.[7]

LIFE FORMS: Antarctica is the harshest place on Earth. The largest terrestrial inhabitant (one spending its entire life on land) is a midge, a wingless flylike insect one-half inch (1.25 centimeters) long. Even in the warmest regions of the Antarctic Peninsula there are only two species of flowering plants and a few species of insects. Other terrestrial life is limited to primitive organisms such as bacteria, yeast, and lichens, all of which have been identified within 300 miles (482 kilometers) of the South Pole. About one hundred kinds of fish live in the ocean around Antarctica, which abounds with tiny, shrimplike *krill* that feed on microscopic floating plants. Many kinds of whales migrate to the Antarctic for the summer to feed on krill. Several kinds of penguins, and many kinds of seals, breed on the coasts and islands but spend most of their lives in the water. About forty kinds of flying birds visit the Antarctic in the summer.

Set at the most southerly
point of land that can be
reached regularly by ship,
McMurdo Station, on Ross
Island, is the center for the
U.S. Antarctic Research
Program.

During the earlier period of research, scientists focused on understanding the Antarctic itself. The inward look was understandable. As late as 1950, Antarctica remained the most mysterious land on Earth. More than half of the continent had never been explored.

But antarctic science has evolved in scope, and now looks outward to the rest of the Earth, and deep into the universe. It focuses on using the Antarctic to understand much broader scientific problems. The research still helps to expand knowledge about Antarctica. But it also has important applications elsewhere, in understanding global processes like climate change, ocean levels, the effects of industrial pollutants, and even the origin and fate of the universe.

Antarctica, in this sense, has become modern science's version of a "canary-in-a-cage," an early-warning system for detecting global environmental change. Coal miners once carried cages of the tiny yellow birds underground as sensors to detect poisonous gas. If a canary died, the miners dropped their picks and shovels and scrambled to the surface. Likewise, modern studies of antarctic organisms are providing early information about the damaging effects of ozone depletion. The *ozone hole*, a thinning of the atmospheric layer that protects Earth from the sun's *ultraviolet light*, was discovered in Antarctica. Other studies of the massive West Antarctic Ice Sheet are helping to establish worldwide consequences of another global environmental threat, the *greenhouse effect*. This warming of Earth's climate is caused by a buildup of carbon dioxide and other gases in the *atmosphere* that blocks the release of Earth's heat. If global warming should melt polar ice sheets, sea levels would rise, flooding many coastal areas.

Scientists also are establishing the global importance of the southern ocean, formed by the South Atlantic, South Pacific, and Indian oceans, which surround the Antarctic. The southern ocean contains only about 10 percent of Earth's water.[1] But exchanges of heat, water, and gas between the ocean and the atmosphere influence global weather and regulate the world's climate.

The Antarctic even serves as a time machine that scientists can use to glimpse conditions that existed during remote periods in the planet's history. Dinosaur bones and fossilized trees have been discovered there, remnants of a time millions of years ago when there was no ice sheet and a milder climate prevailed. Geological studies show that Antarctica once was part of an ancient supercontinent, Gondwanaland. The continent began to break up 180 million years ago. Continental drift, the movement of big plates of rock that make up Earth's surface, divided it into what is now Africa, South America, India, New Zealand, and Australia. Some evidence suggests that Antarctica and Texas once were neighbors 800 million years ago, before continental drift broke them apart.[2] Geologists have found that rock layers in the Shackleton Range bear striking similarities to those in the southwestern United States. The Antarctic's ice, which averages over 6,400 feet (1,950 meters) in thickness, also is an archive of Earth's climatic history. By drilling into the ice and extracting and studying cores, scientists can reconstruct climatic conditions going back more than 250,000 years.

The Antarctic is also a window on the universe, with major astronomical research programs being conducted at the South Pole. Indeed, one ongoing program uses the polar ice cap as a detector for *neutrinos*. Neutrinos are mysterious subatomic particles from space that pass unnoticed through you, me, and everything on Earth. Conditions at the South Pole are ideal for the program's neutrino detectors, which monitor neutrinos that have entered Earth from the North Pole and passed through the entire planet. The South Pole is the best place on Earth for astronomers to conduct other studies, and the *only* place where some can be done.

In addition to helping humanity explore Earth and the universe, antarctic science may prepare men and women for

A researcher prepares to go under the ice with a camera and sampling equipment.

The Amundsen-Scott South Pole Station is cut off from the world for eight months of the year, during the long antarctic winter.

actual exploration of other worlds. In the early 1990s the National Aeronautics and Space Administration (NASA) explored using the Antarctic to train personnel and test equipment for manned missions to Mars and other planets. The Antarctic is so remote, so cold, so dry, so hostile that it can be used to simulate conditions that astronauts would encounter on other planets.

Come along now for a more detailed look at the world's biggest and most exciting laboratory, a continent made for science: Antarctica.

ON PENGUIN ISLAND

Our raftlike Zodiac plows through the choppy gray water of Arthur Harbor on the Antarctic Peninsula, 600 miles (966 kilometers) from the tip of South America. The scientists aboard huddle with faces cast down to avoid fumes of outboard motor exhaust and the saltwater spray. The water is 28°F (−2°C), and the spray stings like needles. As we approach Torgersen Island, a powerful odor sweeps over the inflated rubber boat. Imagine a zoo building where lions or monkeys are housed. Then imagine an odor of animal feces a hundred times stronger.

That's the smell of 15,744 penguins, crammed into a nesting area that seems little larger than a football field. From a distance, the ground appears to be covered in faint pink. It is a carpet of penguin droppings, slightly reddish from the animals' diet of krill. The little Adélie penguins let out a din of warbling, waddling and flapping their flippers in complaint as the scientists disembark and walk between their nests. We walk carefully; the rock-strewn ground is slippery with fresh feces. It also is littered with the decaying bodies of penguins that died during last year's nesting season.

Mention the word "laboratory," and most people think of scientists in spotless white coats, working in sterile labs with test tubes, microscopes, and delicate scientific instruments. But Torgersen Island is another kind of laboratory, a living labora-

Facing page: Adélie penguins seem unconcerned by the presence of this researcher. They've had ample opportunity to grow used to scientists, who study almost every aspect of their behavior.

tory in Antarctica. There, as at some other sites, the research itself can be a shock for people who think of science as a clean and tidy pursuit.

STUDYING AN ECOSYSTEM

The penguins on Torgersen Island, and at other nesting sites, or "rookeries," are objects of one of the most important continuing research programs ever conducted in Antarctica. Called the Long Term Environmental Research (LTER) program, it is an effort to improve scientific understanding of the antarctic *ecosystem* near Palmer Station, America's main research facility on the Antarctic Peninsula. The study's findings may also have global implications.

An ecosystem is a community that consists of all the living organisms in a particular area, plus the sunlight, water, climate and other non-living elements in the region. Unlike other parts of Antarctica, the region around Palmer Station is well suited for studying ecosystem interactions. It is warm enough to support a wider variety of living things than any other part of Antarctica. Scientists accustomed to working at the South Pole and other very cold regions sometimes exaggerate and call this the "Banana Belt" of the Antarctic.

Adélie penguins were selected for the LTER because their survival may indicate the overall condition of their ecosystem—and much more. Penguins are near the top of their ecosystem's *food chain*. Biologists believe that all the living things in an ecosystem are linked by what they eat, and they use the term "food chain" to refer to this interdependence. The beginning of any food chain—the first link, as it were—is an area's plant life. Only plants can produce food through *photosynthesis*. During this process, plants use sunlight, water, and carbon dioxide to produce chemical nutrients and oxygen. An ecosystem's animals live by eating its plants, becoming what scientists call primary consumers. These animals may then be eaten by other animals, called secondary consumers, which, in turn, may be eaten by a third or tertiary set of consumers. An ecosystem may have many food chains. They often overlap, branch out, and interconnect, forming what ecologists term a *food web.*

In the ecosystem surrounding Palmer Station, the food chain is short and simple. Algae and other microscopic ocean plants, *phytoplankton,* are the foundation. Krill feed on these plants. Penguins are the next link. All their energy for breathing, waddling, swimming, and reproducing comes from eating the krill. While swimming in the ocean to catch krill, penguins sometimes fall prey to leopard seals. These big, spotted seals are one link above penguins in the antarctic food chain.

WARNING SIGNS OF GLOBAL CHANGE

Scientists believe that changes in the food chain around Palmer Station may influence the Adélie's survival. These changes may also reflect the state of the local ecosystem and perhaps even Earth's environment. At the outset of the LTER, researchers already had some evidence that increased ultraviolet light (UV) from the sun was damaging antarctic krill. UV consists of invisible rays that, in moderate amounts, are responsible for suntan and sunburn in humans. Excessive exposure to UV can cause skin cancer and other problems. UV increases are believed to result from a buildup of pollutants that deplete Earth's protective *ozone layer.* The ozone layer, located high in the atmosphere, shields Earth's surface from UV rays.

Could the effects of planetary pollution be seen in these tiny, shrimp-like creatures? One method of looking for krill damage in the LTER involved what sometimes was referred to as "puking" the penguins. Scientists *did* have a technical term for obtaining the stomach contents of these sea birds with tuxedo-like markings and waddling walk: gastric lavage. The procedure involved pouring water down the penguins' throats to fill their stomachs, then pumping stomach contents into buckets. The buckets then went back to the laboratory at Palmer Station, a half mile (0.8 kilometer) across Arthur Harbor.

By analyzing the penguin diet, scientists hoped to spot early signs of UV-induced damage to krill populations. One of the key steps in this analysis involved sorting through the mess of regurgitate. Scientists made a special effort to find krill eyeballs, which are used as an indicator of the size, age, and conditions of krill the Adélies ate.

In early 1994, data on the krill was incomplete. Still, researchers remained convinced that understanding threats to the Adélie food chain and, by extension, the penguin's survival, could lead to an understanding of threats to the global environment.

LOCAL FACTORS

A scientist monitors air quality. Small changes in factors such as air pollution can have major effects on the antarctic environment.

Meanwhile, ongoing LTER studies help scientists to understand other local factors that influence the survival of the Adélies and their ecosystem. The ecosystem around Palmer Station is simple and highly sensitive to the effects of climatic and environmental change. Slight effects not apparent in the more complex ecosystems of North America, for instance, are magnified in the Antarctic's short, simple food chain.

Japanese and Russian fishing trawlers catch large quantities of antarctic krill each year. They process the krill into different seafood products. Their harvest of krill doubled during the 1980s, from about 200,000 tons per year to 500,000 tons.[1] Likewise, human activity, including visits by tour ships, increased in the Palmer Peninsula region during this time. In 1989, the Argentine supply ship *Bahia Parasio* ran aground one mile from Palmer Station. The accident spilled hundreds of thousands of gallons of fuel and lubricating oil into the sea.[2] The chicks of thousands of seabirds were exposed to the oil.

How do krill fishing, oil spills, and other human activities affect antarctic wildlife?

An inflatable
Zodiac packed
with equipment
allows scientists
to test the
antarctic waters,
monitoring subtle
environmental
changes.

(27)

Life Cycles of the Adélie Penguin

In order to spot changes in an animal population caused by environmental or other factors, scientists must know how the animals are born, how they reproduce, and how they die under normal conditions. For LTER scientists, this has meant understanding the life cycles of the Adélies.

A nineteenth-century French explorer, Dumont d'Urville, named the penguins after his dainty wife, Adélie. But the birds are anything but delicate. Although they may look cute and fragile, they are surprisingly tough and sometimes mean—requirements for surviving in the harsh antarctic environment. Many Adélies live fourteen years or more, and most reproduce every year.

The Adélies build nests about 10 inches (25 centimeters) in diameter on the bare ground, using the only available material, small pebbles about an inch in diameter. Unattached males sometimes can be seen waddling through a rookery, waving pebbles in their beaks in the hopes of attracting mates.

As more penguins return to the nesting colony in the spring, almost every pebble is snatched up and used in a nest. Some biologists believe that the pebble supply has an impact on the size of penguin populations. The number of pebbles apparently limits the number of nests that can be built. Penguins that return early get not only lots of pebbles but the best nesting sites in the center of the colony. Central nests, surrounded by many others, are most protected from seagull-like skuas, which eat penguin eggs and newly hatched chicks.

Female penguins usually lay two big brown eggs that hatch within thirty-five to forty days. Parents take turns guarding their nests and diving to bring back krill for their hatchlings. The parents eat the krill, then regurgitate it into a pile at the nest, where the hungry chicks peck it up.

Young Adélies must learn to fend for themselves quickly. Parents provide food only for about seven weeks. The chicks are then on their own to die or survive, and begin the life cycle anew.

These questions lure biologists every year to the living lab on Torgersen Island and to other penguin rookeries. They monitor the Adélies, keeping records on every aspect of the penguins' lives. The work begins in the nesting season in October, early in the antarctic spring. The Adélies leave their winter quarters at the edge of the sea ice, and return to the rocky shores of Torgersen Island to breed and raise chicks. Scientists want to know how many penguins return each year. So they do a census, counting the number of penguins nesting at

An Adélie penguin and chick, on their nest of stones.

Once banded, this Adélie penguin will be released unharmed.

Torgersen. A decrease in the number of nesting penguins could indicate a natural fluctuation due to severe winter conditions. But it also could signal an environmental problem resulting from pollution or other human activities.

Scientists conduct intensive studies on samples of the penguin population. Several hundred of these birds are banded, for instance. Scientists slide a small aluminum identification tag around the base of one flipper. Teams of field researchers carefully monitor the activities of these penguins. They take great care to avoid harming or disturbing the animals, especially during nesting. Many of the observations are done from a distance, with binoculars. Researchers keep a close eye on the comings and goings of the banded penguins. Studies have shown that the ID bands do not interfere with the penguins' activities.

In addition to watching and taking notes on the Adélies, researchers also use automated monitoring devices. Some of the penguins are rigged with battery-operated recorders. The device weighs about 2 ounces (56.7 grams) and is fastened to a strip of Velcro. The strip attaches to the penguin's back, and falls off harmlessly when the animal molts, or sheds its feathers. The device records the depth of each dive the penguin takes while feeding, and the length of time it remains submerged. The typical penguin makes about seventy-five dives during a feeding trip. It remains submerged for up to two minutes and may reach depths of almost 300 feet (91 meters). Researchers remove the recorder after a penguin returns to the nest, and transfer the data to a computer.

Scientists conducting the LTER also study other organisms lower down in the food chain. These include krill eaten by penguins, antarctic silverfish eaten by skua, and the algae that anchor the food chain. They are especially interested in environmental factors in the local ecosystem that affect the food supply—and survival—of all these organisms.

More LTER work remains to be done before scientists really know what the success of these penguins implies about their immediate surroundings and our world as a whole. One thing is clear. Research at sites such as Torgersen Island is proving that Antarctica is a place of paradox, a vast wasteland that is also a rich source of information we have yet to fully understand.

UNDER THE OZONE HOLE

In 1983, British scientists stumbled onto a mystery about the atmosphere over Antarctica. They had carefully monitored gases in the atmosphere over their research base at Halley Bay since the 1970s. Now a scientist named Joseph C. Farman was examining the results. He found that a critical gas called *ozone* was mysteriously disappearing. Ozone is a form of oxygen that blocks harmful rays from the sun. Farman's evidence suggested that the amount of ozone in the atmosphere had decreased by more than 40 percent since 1977.[1] Unable to believe his own data, he spent months confirming the observations.

Over a vast area of Antarctica, Farman later concluded, levels of protective ozone in the atmosphere were falling sharply every spring. So much ozone was disappearing that it seemed like a "hole" had opened in the ozone layer. The hole was not actually a hole, but a region of the atmosphere depleted or deficient in ozone. Reduced ozone levels in the hole were allowing more ultraviolet rays to pour through. Farman and the other members of his team announced discovery of the antarctic ozone hole in 1985. It had a major impact in helping people recognize ozone depletion as a real environmental threat.

The discovery turned Antarctica into a laboratory for studying how ozone depletion might affect people, animals, and plants around the world. Scientists began to realize that Antarctica could serve as a kind of time machine for determining the future effects of ozone depletion; the severe depletion that some scientists expected to occur over North America in the twenty-first century was already happening in the Antarctic. How did ozone depletion affect plant and animal life? Could organisms learn to protect themselves from high levels of ultraviolet light coming through the hole?

There was no better place on Earth for answering these questions than the frozen continent. Ozone depletion has become one of the major areas of antarctic research. Like other research projects, it provides information about Antarctica. But the information also is important for the rest of the world. Since the first intensive studies of antarctic ozone began in 1986, researchers have determined why an ozone hole forms and have gained many clues about its effects on life.

AN ODD PLACE FOR CLOUDS

American scientists quickly confirmed Farman's discovery. They looked at data on antarctic ozone levels gathered by a *Nimbus 7* satellite, which also showed an ozone hole opening in the atmosphere over Antarctica. Evidence indicated that the hole begins to form right after winter darkness ends and the first rays of sunlight reach the Antarctic in September. Ozone depletion gradually intensifies and reaches a peak in October. The hole remains in place until November, and then disappears as ozone levels return to normal.

Why does sunrise raise the curtain on such severe ozone depletion? Why don't ozone holes open in other parts of the atmosphere? Why does the antarctic ozone hole disappear in November? Scientists conducted a wide range of studies in an effort to understand these mysteries.

Researchers monitored the appearance, development, and disappearance of the ozone hole with detectors on the ground, in balloons drifting through the atmosphere, and with satellites orbiting Earth. They flew into different regions of the ozone hole in specially equipped aircraft, including a research version of the U-2 spy plane. They amassed detailed information about chemical reactions, atmospheric gases, weather conditions, movements of air masses, and other factors that affect the hole. From this information they were able to develop a theory of why the ozone hole forms over Antarctica, and why it behaves so strangely.

Most scientists believe that ozone thins over Antarctica because winter temperatures are low enough for an odd kind of cloud to form. This type of cloud is odd because it forms in the stratosphere. Scientists once regarded stratospheric clouds as extremely rare because this part of the atmosphere seemed far too dry and warm for clouds. The stratosphere contains about a thousand times less water vapor than the troposphere, the bottom layer of air where most weather occurs.[2] Although the stratosphere is high above the earth, it is surprisingly warm. Temperatures there actually *increase* with altitude, reaching about 28°F (−2°C) at the upper levels.[3] Temperatures in the troposphere, in contrast, decrease with altitude, and may be as low as −112°F (−80°C).[4]

Despite the extremely dry air, scientists found that winter temperatures in the stratosphere over Antarctica drop low enough for clouds to form. These polar stratospheric clouds consist of microscopic ice crystals. The crystals provide the surfaces—the nooks and crannies—on which chlorofluorocarbons (CFCs) interact with sunlight to destroy ozone in an extremely rapid fashion. (Stratospheric clouds also form over the North Pole. But ozone depletion there is less serious because temperatures are higher, and fewer clouds can form.)

Wind patterns over Antarctica are another important factor in formation of the ozone hole. These winds, called the circumpolar vortex, become established in the Antarctic each winter. They blow in a circular pattern, the circumference of which acts like a wall that isolates the continent. Air from surrounding areas cannot pass through the wall of the vortex. Antarctica thus becomes sealed off. Ozone in the surrounding atmosphere cannot flow in to replace depleted ozone. So the depletion increases.

How Ozone Is Created and Destroyed

Most of the world's ozone occurs in a layer in the *stratosphere*, a level of Earth's atmosphere that begins at an altitude of about 10 miles (16 kilometers) and ends at about 30 miles (48 kilometers). Ozone forms there when sunlight collides with molecules of oxygen that have drifted up from below. Ordinary oxygen, the kind we breathe, consists of a *molecule*, a group of atoms chemically bonded together. The molecule has two oxygen atoms. Sunlight in the stratosphere rips the oxygen molecule apart, releasing the atoms. They quickly recombine to make a form of oxygen with three atoms. This triple oxygen molecule is ozone. Ozone is constantly being created and destroyed. Sunlight also rips ozone molecules apart into oxygen atoms. Most recombine into new ozone. The ozone then interacts with sunlight, breaks apart, and reforms. (Don't confuse this protective *stratospheric* ozone with the harmful ozone that forms at ground level during hot summer weather. Often mentioned on news broadcasts during air-pollution alerts, ground-level ozone forms as a result of automobile exhaust and other air pollutants. It has a number of bad effects on people and crop plants.)

In 1974, Mario J. Molina and F. Sherwood Rowland discovered that atmospheric ozone was being destroyed. These American scientists, who worked at the University of California at Irvine, reported that certain industrial chemicals could deplete the ozone layer. The chemicals are gases called *chlorofluorocarbons* (CFCs). CFCs were used since the 1930s to cool refrigerators and air conditioners. They had other uses, such as forcing aerosol sprays out of cans and in making foam plastics such as seat cushions and packaging material. By 1974, more than 850,000 million pounds of CFCs were produced in the United States each year.[9] The CFCs were released into the atmosphere, and rose into the stratosphere. Molina and Rowland showed that chlorine from CFCs destroyed ozone. Strong sunlight in the stratosphere tore molecules of CFC apart, releasing atoms of chlorine. (As the name *chloro/fluoro/carbon* suggests, CFCs consist of atoms of chlorine, fluorine, and carbon.) Scientists calculated that a single chlorine atom reaching the stratosphere could destroy 100,000 ozone molecules.[10]

In 1978, the United States banned the use of CFCs in aerosol cans, but little was done to control other uses of CFCs because the threat was underestimated. Joseph Farman's discovery of the antarctic ozone hole made the threat real, and set the stage for further action against CFCs. With such clear evidence of CFCs' effects, twenty-four nations in 1987 signed an international agreement to reduce production and use of CFCs and other ozone-depleting industrial chemicals by 1999. The nations accounted for about 99 percent of the world's production of CFCs, and 90 percent of their use.[11] The agreement, called the Montreal Protocol on Substances That Deplete the Ozone Layer, went into effect in 1989. More than seventy countries have agreed to the Montreal Protocol. In 1992, the United States announced that it would end production of CFCs by December 31, 1995, sooner than many other countries.

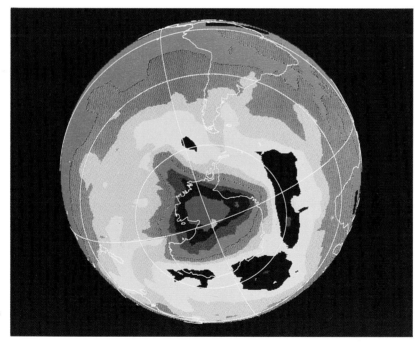

In a computer image of the antarctic "ozone hole," blues and purples show where the ozone layer is thin.

By spring sunrise, the stage is set for formation of the ozone hole. Stratospheric clouds have formed during the frigid winter. The circumpolar vortex is in place. Rays of sunlight are ready to play their role in the chemical reactions that destroy ozone. The ozone hole disappears by November because temperatures increase enough to melt the stratospheric clouds. Likewise, the winter circumpolar vortex breaks down, allowing ozone-rich air to flow in. Big "pools" of ozone-depleted air, the remains of the hole, may drift through the Southern Hemisphere. Ozone from the surrounding air flows into them, reducing average ozone levels throughout the Southern Hemisphere.

On a chart showing ozone depletion, a scientist indicates the extent of the ozone hole in October 1992. It was larger than Antarctica.

The ozone hole varies in size, but often is huge—larger than the continental United States. The 1992 ozone hole covered an area of 9.4 million square miles (24.3 million square kilometers).[5] It was bigger than the entire surface area of Antarctica. The 1993 ozone hole covered 9 million square miles.[6] The ozone hole formed every other year in the late 1980s. But in the early 1990s, it formed every year. Ozone depletion in the hole has also become more severe. The ozone hole that formed late in 1993, for instance, had the lowest levels of ozone ever recorded on Earth. Scientists believe that the low levels were due, in part, to chemicals released by the eruption of the Mount Pinatubo volcano in 1991 in the Philippines. These natural chemicals can also deplete atmospheric ozone.

BLIND RABBITS AND TWO-HEADED SHEEP

In some years, the antarctic ozone hole gets big enough to cause concern in the nearest populated areas. In 1990, for instance, scientists discovered that the ozone hole reached the lower part of South America. It covered Punta Arenas, Chile, the southernmost large city on Earth, which has a population of about 120,000. People in the city became concerned about the risk of skin cancer and of eye problems from the strong UV light coming through the hole. They took extra care to wear sun block and sunglasses.

Rumors began to circulate of strange biological effects from overexposure to the UV rays. Hunters claimed that rabbits had gone blind and could be captured by hand. Ranchers thought the UV rays had burned their sheep's eyes. Some people claimed to have seen two-headed sheep or plants that supposedly were mutated—genetically changed—by UV rays. A few physicians suspected that humans were suffering more skin cancer and eye problems. Scientists from Johns Hopkins University in Baltimore, Maryland, and the Chilean Ministry of Health investigated. Their report, issued in 1993, could find no sign, as yet, that the ozone hole caused any harm to animals or people in Punta Arenas. The experts concluded that the eye problems in the area's sheep were actually due to a virus. They could find no evidence of mutated animals and plants.

Scientists are, however, finding early indications that the more severe ozone depletion over the Antarctic does harm some organisms. Some of the clearest evidence came from a major research expedition conducted in 1990 by teams of scientists from the University of California at Santa Barbara, Scripps Institution of Oceanography in San Diego, the University of Hawaii, and the University of California at San Francisco. Oceanographers Raymond Smith and Barbara Prezelin, of the University of California at Santa Barbara, were in charge of the project.

The scientists spent six weeks aboard the R/V *Polar Duke*, a specially equipped research vessel that can steam through ice-clogged seas. The expedition coincided with the springtime appearance of the ozone hole. While the *Polar Duke* cruised in the Bellingshausen Sea in the Antarctic Peninsula, the scientists conducted a variety of studies. They lowered sensors into the water, for instance, to measure UV penetration at various depths. They measured how currents move plankton through the water. Then they scooped up samples of different kinds of phytoplankton to measure their productivity, the rate at which plankton grow and produce energy and food with photosynthesis—a barometer of plankton health. They compared productivity in whole communities of plankton.

A researcher checks a tank of krill. The tiny crustaceans are being studied to find out how they are affected by ultra-violet radiation.

Some were under the ozone hole, and getting high levels of UV light. Others were away from the hole, getting normal levels of UV. Scientists checked plankton for signs of genetic damage from UV light.

The team's findings, announced in 1992, represented a landmark in efforts to understand the biological effects of the ozone hole. The scientists found clear evidence that phytoplankton production decreased by at least 6 to 12 percent during the antarctic spring, when ozone depletion is most severe.[7] The discovery was disturbing because decreased growth of plankton could mean less food available for krill, and for animals, such as penguins, that eat krill. The expedition also reported that phytoplankton can defend themselves from UV damage, and even repair damage that does occur. Phytoplankton can make sunblocklike chemicals, and use other chemicals to reverse genetic damage from UV. But phytoplankton differ in their ability to do so. Least able to cope with strong UV, for instance, were the most common phytoplankton, which make up most of the phytoplankton eaten by krill.

ENDURING QUESTIONS

Ozone depletion occurs not just in the Antarctic, but around the world. In 1993, for instance, scientists with the National Oceanic and Atmospheric Administration (NOAA) reported that ozone levels over the United States had fallen to unusually low levels. The concentrations were 5 to 18 percent below normal levels observed during the previous twenty years.[8]

People increasingly look to antarctic research for information about the health and other biological effects of ozone depletion. Research already has brought some reassurance that an ozone hole may not form over the United States. Many scientists believe that an ozone hole requires unique conditions that may exist only in the Antarctic. Research has also offered reassurance that living things may be able to adapt to higher UV levels.

Still, many questions endure. Many answers may, however, be found in the living UV laboratory that stratospheric clouds and the circumpolar vortex have created in Antarctica.

A HOT PLACE
FOR
ASTRONOMY

Ask any astronomer to list his or her requirements for a paradise on Earth, a place where conditions are ideal for observing celestial objects. All would want a high-altitude site, above the murky, turbulent air near ground level that blurs images of stars, in a place that has dry, cloud-free weather. Most would want a site that's dark twenty-four hours a day, where they could observe heavenly objects for months at a time, rather than just for a few hours a night. Some even might want to stop the nightly rising and setting of stars and constellations, keeping celestial objects constantly visible in the sky. Solar astronomers, who study the sun, would want to stop its daily setting, so they could continue their studies without interruption. Radio astronomers, who study radio-type signals from space, might want to prohibit the use of every automobile, hair drier, and other source of electronic "noise" for miles around.

Such a haven for astronomy actually does exist on Earth. It is the South Pole region of Antarctica. The South Pole combines so many desirable characteristics for astronomy that it is the world's best site for many kinds of observations. Indeed, for certain studies, telescopes at the South Pole are more sensitive than the Hubble Space Telescope, which orbits Earth. Orbiting instruments in satellites, or on the space shuttle, can cost tens or hundreds of millions of dollars, moreover. Antarctica is so much cheaper that it is sometimes called "the poor man's space shuttle."

Good viewing conditions always have existed at the South Pole, but scientists have just begun to take advantage of the conditions. An American physicist named Martin Pomerantz recognized the South Pole's potential for astronomy after going there in 1957 during the International Geophysical Year. He told many other scientists about the good viewing conditions.

In 1979, Pomerantz and a Swedish scientist brought a small telescope to the South Pole. They used it to study changes in the sun's production of energy. The results made them even more enthusiastic about astronomy at the South Pole. They returned the next summer for more research, and continued promoting the South Pole as a good place for astronomy. Gradually, other astronomers began to recognize the advantages of doing their observations in this desolate land.

CARA, AST/RO, SPIREX, COBRA

In 1991, the National Science Foundation decided to establish a major astronomical observatory at the South Pole. It is called the Center for Astrophysical Research in Antarctica (CARA). The University of Chicago's Yerkes Observatory operates CARA, but scientists from a number of other universities and research centers are involved in the project.

CARA consists of three telescopes with the potential for answering questions about the origin of the universe, how stars and planets are born, and other cosmic mysteries.

One telescope is called the Antarctic Submillimeter Telescope and Remote Observatory (AST/RO). It is a 1.7-meter (5.6-foot) telescope for detecting "submillimeter" radiation. Stars and other objects emit a wide range, or spectrum, of electromagnetic rays or radiation. Visible light makes up only a small portion of this *electromagnetic spectrum*. Radiation in the spectrum travels through space in waves that vary in length.

A researcher is dwarfed
by this massive solar
telescope, which can be
used to study the sun
twenty-four hours a day
in the antarctic summer.

*At the
South Pole,
a telescope
points skyward
in search of
cosmic micro-
wave radiation.*

(46)

Submillimeter rays travel at a wavelength of less than a millimeter, about the thickness of a paperclip.

AST/RO is intended to scan immense clouds of gas and dust that emit submillimeter radiation in central parts of the Milky Way Galaxy, the system of 100 million to 200 million stars in which Earth is located. Astronomers believe that in these centers, stars are being born. They hope AST/RO's images will allow them to peek into the "stellar nurseries," glimpse newborn stars, and observe their early stages of life. In doing so, the scientists will glean valuable information about the nuclear reactions and other processes needed to create stars.

The second telescope is the South Pole Infrared Explorer (SPIREX). Its purpose is to detect *infrared radiation* from galaxies formed when the universe was very young. This radiation was released immense distances from Earth, and has taken many billions of years to travel across the universe. It thus remains visible to astronomers. Because of the South Pole's excellent viewing conditions, SPIREX can provide better images of this kind of radiation than the Hubble Telescope. Astronomers use SPIREX in efforts to answer some of the most enduring questions about the origins of the universe.

The third telescope is the Cosmic Background Radiation Anisotropy telescope (COBRA). *Anisotropy* is a term that describes irregularities or variations in something that otherwise is uniform. COBRA searches for and maps small variations in the cosmic microwave background radiation. This is the original radiation left over from the *Big Bang*. The Big Bang theory proposes that the universe originated from a tiny but unimaginably dense particle of pure energy. About 15 billion years ago, for some reason, the particle exploded. It filled space with radiation and atomic particles that changed into gas. As billions of years passed, gravity compressed the gas into the raw material for stars, galaxies, planets, and everything else in the universe—even you and me.

Astronomers developed the Big Bang theory in the 1920s. It got a big boost in 1965, when astronomers discovered the

Stones From the Sky

Some astronomers in Antarctica do more than gaze at celestial objects. They actually collect pieces of comets, asteroids, the moon, and Mars. These stones from the heavens are *meteorites*. Meteorites are pieces of extraterrestrial material that survive a fiery plunge through the atmosphere and land intact on Earth's surface.

Just as conditions in Antarctica are ideal for viewing celestial objects, they also are great for collecting them. The antarctic ice sheet acts like a trap that collects and preserves meteorites.

After a meteorite lands on a glacier, it sinks below the surface, where the ice "flows" much like a river. These ice streams may flow several hundred feet a year, carrying the meteorites. Eventually, the stream flows into a mountain or rocky terrain that forces it upward. Meteorites buried in the ice rise to the surface. Fierce winds erode the remaining ice, uncovering the meteorites. Some have been preserved, frozen in their original condition, for millions of years.

Each summer, teams of scientists from the United States and other countries set up remote camps on the Beardmore Glacier. Field-team members spend about six weeks riding snowmobiles to search hilly areas where ice streams rise to the surface.

The searches have been a spectacular success. Japanese geologists discovered the first nine antarctic meteorites in 1969. Since then, astronomers have found more than 16,000 meteorites in the Antarctic.[1] This is more meteorites than have been found in all the rest of the world. Antarctic meteorites include many previously unknown types, and tend to be more ancient. Among them are bits of rock with the same chemical composition as lunar samples returned by the Apollo space missions. Scientists think that other meteorites may be fragments from Mars.

Astronomers believe that such meteorites originate when meteors smashed into the moon or planets like Mars. The impact hurled debris into space toward Earth. Other meteorites may be the remains of comets or asteroids. Some are believed to be material left over from the formation of the solar system 4.5 billion years ago. Antarctic meteorites give astronomers a rare opportunity for hands-on study of the composition of other celestial bodies and formation of the solar system.

cosmic background radiation, the relic radiation left over from the Big Bang. Key evidence, however, was still missing. The radiation seemed to be uniform across the sky. But gravity could form stars and constellations only if "lumps" were present—irregular areas of matter denser than their surroundings. Gravity in these irregular dense areas, or anisotropies, would draw matter together so it could congeal into stars and other objects. In 1992 astronomers reported evidence that these denser areas do exist. They used images taken with the Cosmic Background Explorer (COBE) satellite to detect radiation from ancient "structures." The structures were huge, dense regions in space—irregularities that developed just after the universe was born.

The South Pole's COBRA telescope is designed to observe structures in the early universe smaller than those that can be detected with COBE. Using a prototype version of the telescope, astronomers at the South Pole discovered evidence of what may be the very first structures that formed in the universe. They believe that the dense areas eventually developed into galaxies that populate the universe today.

BIG BANG AND BIG CRUNCH

Another South Pole astronomical instrument called the Antarctic Muon and Neutrino Array (AMANDA) may help determine the ultimate fate of the universe. The Big Bang hurtled all matter in the universe outward from the central point of creation. Astronomers know that the universe is expanding, with all objects moving away from each other.

Will the universe expand forever? If so, some say stars and galaxies will continue moving farther and farther apart. As billions of years pass, stars will burn out, and life on their orbiting planets will vanish. Finally, nothing but darkness will remain.

Some astronomers, however, say the expansion will stop, and the Big Bang will be followed by the Big Crunch (also called the Big Squeeze). Proponents of the Big Crunch theory argue that stars and galaxies will expand to a certain point. Then, like a punctured balloon, the universe will collapse. All stars and planets and other matter will hurtle back in toward a central point. Everything will mash and crunch together. Next comes one of the most fascinating possibilities. Some believe that when the universe crunches back down to a speck of pure energy, a new Big Bang will create a new universe and life will emerge anew. Indeed, billions of years in the future, there may be a new version of Earth, with a new version of you and me.

Scientists believe that much depends on the amount of matter in the universe. Astronomers calculate that if there is enough matter, gravity will be strong enough to eventually halt the universe's expansion. But estimates of the amount of matter visible from Earth indicate that there is not nearly enough matter to stop the expansion. Indeed, astronomers can account for barely 1 percent of the necessary amount. Many astronomers believe that the universe has much more matter than can be seen from Earth. They call it "dark matter" because it is invisible.

Neutrinos may be the key to identifying this invisible matter. Neutrinos are ghostly subatomic particles that can pass through all solid material as if it did not exist. Even if Earth were a ball of solid lead, neutrinos would zip right through. Trillions pass unnoticed through your body every minute. At night, neutrinos from the sun shining on the other side of the world pass right through Earth before zipping through you.

Neutrinos also are produced in distant celestial objects such as *neutron stars* and *black holes*. Neutron stars are believed to be incredibly dense objects left over when stars explode. All the matter in the star is packed into a sphere only about 12 miles (19 kilometers) in diameter. Black holes also are believed to be the remains of collapsed stars. They are so dense, and have such powerful gravity, that nothing, not even light can escape. The gravity pulls everything inward.

Some astronomers believe that objects like black holes may make up much of the invisible matter in the universe.

Astronomers hope that by detecting neutrinos, they can trace the neutrinos' paths back to previously unknown invisible objects like black holes. In doing so, they may identify enough dark matter to determine whether the universe will expand forever or crunch inward.

AMANDA, THE NEUTRINO TELESCOPE

AMANDA may help to finally identify the universe's missing mass. Muons are particles formed when neutrinos interact with matter. AMANDA's purpose is to detect these interactions. The telescope consists of a series of electronic detectors placed inside holes bored more than a half mile into the antarctic ice cap near the South Pole. The holes were actually melted in the ice with hot water squirted from high-pressure hoses. The deep ice screens out interference from other cosmic particles that shower the Earth.

The antarctic ice cap likewise is big enough and clear enough for detectors to pick up the neutrinos' telltale flashes of light. There is no limit to the size of an ice-cap detector, since any amount of ice can be rigged with electronic instruments and used as a neutrino telescope. AMANDA, still under construction in 1994, was to be fifty times bigger than any existing neutrino telescope. Perhaps it will help answer our most basic questions concerning our origins.

OTHER MYSTERIES

Other kinds of astronomical research are also done at the South Pole, including projects to determine the source of *cosmic rays*. Cosmic rays are mysterious, high-energy particles from outer space that constantly bombard Earth's upper atmosphere. Although cosmic rays were discovered in 1911, astronomers still do not know their source. Some believe that cosmic rays are produced by exploding stars, black holes, and other celestial objects. The South Pole Air Shower Experiment (SPASE) is trying to determine the source of cosmic rays. When a cosmic ray strikes the atmosphere, it creates a "shower" of secondary particles that astronomers can detect. With such good conditions at the South Pole, astronomers can watch the same region of the sky for months at a time in an effort to trace the paths of cosmic rays back to their sources. Astronomers also study cosmic rays with detectors lofted high into the atmosphere by huge helium-filled balloons. Because of antarctic wind patterns and stable air, the balloons remain at a constant altitude and travel in a circular path that brings them back toward their launch point.

These research projects, and others, already have established the South Pole as a major center for astronomy. Astronomers are moving ahead with plans for additional projects, bigger telescopes, and more sensitive detectors. They hope that America's Amundsen-Scott South Pole Station will be transformed into a major world center for astronomy. Doing so would not require hundreds of astronomers to make an expensive voyage to the South Pole. Rather, scientists hope telescopes and other instruments can be highly automated, so that astronomers can control them, and see images of objects they detect, with computer terminals in their own offices.

Many research projects at the South Pole also involve international cooperation, with scientists from different countries joining forces to do their research. An opportunity to build an international astronomy center may come late in the 1990s, as the Amundsen-Scott Station is modernized and enlarged to provide more space for research.

Observatories at the South Pole never will replace the big telescopes at Kitt Peak in Arizona, Mauna Kea in Hawaii, and other warm-weather sites. The Antarctic is, after all, difficult to reach and hostile to work in. Its view is limited to celestial objects in the southern portion of the sky. Observing conditions are not always ideal. In winter, for instance, the polar stratospheric clouds that cause the ozone hole can interfere with observations. For most astronomical studies, viewing conditions are not as good as space vehicles hundreds of miles above the Earth—or observatories that may be built on the moon. But South Pole astronomy almost certainly will continue to make a bigger and bigger contribution to our understanding of the origin and fate of the universe.

5

MARS ON EARTH

A spiderlike robot with eight metal legs and electronic eyes in its feet crawls over a lifeless, rock-strewn landscape. It approaches the rim of a huge crater where steam and harsh volcanic gases hiss from vents in the rock. Volcanic eruptions spew molten lava and hot rocks out of the lava pool inside the crater. Some of these flying "lava bombs" are the size of a compact car.

As scientists working for the National Aeronautics and Space Administration (NASA) watch on television monitors in a distant control center, the robot advances. Its orders come through a leashlike tether attached to an eight-wheeled "autonomous land vehicle." The vehicle resembles something from the movie *Star Wars*. The robot, named Dante, inches ahead on its mission, which is to snatch a sample of the corrosive gases spewing from the volcano.

No, this is not a scene from the exploration of another planet, in some future era. It is a scene from Antarctica, the place in this world most like the hostile environments waiting to be explored on Mars and other planets. The tests of Dante were conducted at the Mount Erebus volcano near McMurdo Station, in terrain and conditions that are so harsh that they can serve as a proving ground for equipment and personnel destined for planetary missions.

Facing page: Antarctica's dry valley region, in Victoria Land, is the world's driest desert. Conditions are so severe that the climate is more like that of Mars than Earth.

Antarctica has served as a testing site for simulating or imitating alien environments since the 1960s. American scientists searched the world for a natural environment to test experiments being developed for the Viking spacecraft. Viking 1 and Viking 2 were identical unmanned ships that blasted off from Earth in 1975 on an epic journey to Mars. Their main mission: Search for signs of life on the mysterious Red Planet. The vehicles landed on Mars in 1976, scooped up samples of the rusty red soil, and analyzed it in miniature automated laboratories. At first, the experiments gave tantalizing hints that bacteria or other forms of life existed in the Martian soil. Most experts later agreed that the results were inconclusive. So the question of life on Mars remains unanswered.

But long before the mission, scientists needed to test the experiments in a place with harsh environmental conditions rivaling those on Mars. It had to be extremely cold, dry, devoid of liquid water, shaped by powerful winds, with rugged, rock-strewn terrain. Scientists found Mars on Earth in the Antarctic.

Many conditions unique to the Antarctic made it a perfect Mars analog, or model. When Viking 1 landed 212 million miles (339 million kilometers) from Earth, for instance, it found Martian temperatures like those that occur in the Antarctic. The thermometer in Mars's northern hemisphere dipped to a low of −126 degrees Fahrenheit (−87.78°C), comparable to Earth's record low temperature of −128.6°F, recorded in the Antarctic. Viking 1 occasionally basked in balmy temperatures of −22°F (−30°C), which were equivalent to those on warm summer days at the South Pole. Testing the Viking experiments on Earth under conditions that were closely comparable to those the spacecraft would encounter on Mars gave scientists an idea of Viking's probable success.

In the 1990s, Earth's most Marslike environment began playing another role in testing procedures, equipment, and personnel for a new age in space exploration. It will be an era in which human beings establish a permanent settlement on the moon, and fulfill the age-old dream of setting foot on Mars.

Experts proposed these momentous steps many times in the past. The general outlines of one such mission reappeared in the early 1990s as part of the Space Exploration Initiative (SEI). SEI was a thirty-year U.S. government plan to expand human presence in the solar system beyond Earth. In the first stage of the program, astronauts would build America's first permanent orbiting space station, *Freedom*. During extended space walks, they would assemble *Freedom* from components carried into Earth orbit by the space shuttle. When completed, *Freedom* could serve as a way station for crews departing to other planets. Astronauts would fly to the station aboard the space shuttle, carrying along tons of equipment and supplies in the shuttle's huge cargo bay.

Then, perhaps by the early 2000s, a crew of pioneers would depart for the 240,000-mile (384,000-kilometer) journey to the moon. There they would establish a research outpost that could be expanded into a permanent settlement. Scientists would conduct many experiments that exploit the low gravity and other conditions on the lunar surface. Astronomers would take advantage of the extremely clear viewing conditions and build an observatory on the far side of the moon. Sometime before 2020, another crew would establish an outpost on Mars. They would spend months on the Martian surface, conducting studies to finally resolve age-old questions about the Red Planet, including the existence of life.

PREPARING FOR DANGEROUS MISSIONS

Interplanetary missions would be fraught with dangers unlike those on any previous space flight. Astronauts have always had to function effectively as a tightly-knit unit, in extremely hazardous environments, despite long periods of isolation. But human exploration of the solar system would involve longer periods of isolation, and place crews at greater distances from possible help than ever before. A Mars crew, for instance, would have to live and get along together in cramped quarters for three years—two years spent on the round-trip flight to Mars, and perhaps one year on the Martian surface. They would be away from family, friends, and familiar places.

Researchers have already conducted many studies on how extreme isolation affects the human mind and body. But scientists still do not know exactly what psychological and social traits help individuals adapt to isolation. One problem is that so few people have experienced extreme isolation in the small groups that could travel on space missions. Many questions remain about how small groups of isolated people resolve disagreements and conflict. Space agency officials naturally want to select crews that will be compatible during long missions. Crew members with nasty personalities, bad tempers, or the tendency to use violence to settle disagreements could endanger the entire mission. Information on the effects of isolation will have other critical applications for long-duration space flight. For instance, scientists must find ways of keeping crews mentally alert and ready to deal with unexpected problems. Poor performance by even one crew member could put everyone at risk.

Unmanned planetary missions also require very reliable instruments, since the missions cost hundreds of millions of dollars and repairs are difficult. To assure the safety of human explorers, and the reliable performance of robot devices like Dante, space scientists have turned to the Antarctic. Men and women, instruments and vehicles, have been living and working in its unearthly environment for decades.

ADAPTING TO EXTREME ISOLATION

Antarctic scientists and support personnel, like future planetary explorers, live in extreme isolation in a hostile environment. America's Amundsen-Scott Station at the geographic South

Pole, for instance, is cut off from the rest of the world for eight months of the year. Isolation usually lasts from mid-February until early November. The rugged ski-equipped LC-130 Hercules cargo planes that normally supply the station cannot land and take off during this period. The antarctic night begins in March and does not end until September. Six months of darkness are accompanied by wintertime temperatures that have dipped to −117 degrees F (−83°C). Winds may gust to 40 miles per hour (64 kph). Men and women who remain over the winter must be totally self-sufficient. In the 1960s, the physician at Russia's Vostok Station developed appendicitis and was forced to remove his own appendix. He performed the self-appendectomy with a local anesthetic and mirrors. Similar conditions prevail for the 250 people who remain all winter at America's other research stations.

Antarctic research has provided some reassurance that small groups of people can live happily in extreme isolation. It comes from studies on personnel who "winter over" at the South Pole. Only about twenty-eight people do so each year. During one winter-over period, Dr. Matthew Houseal served as the South Pole physician—the first psychiatrist to do so. He helped to conduct a psychological study on the effects of isolation. The researchers were pleasantly surprised to find that the winter-over crew experienced no serious psychological problems. They could find no link between long isolation from the rest of the world and psychological illness.[1] In fact, the winter-over crew actually found the isolation beneficial. Crew members said it helped them better understand themselves and other people. They learned to be more patient and tolerant of other people, for instance. Some used the time to lose weight or make other changes in their personal lives. All found that the isolation made them appreciate small things in life, such as the taste of fresh fruit and the sight of green plants, that other people take for granted.

Studies in the Antarctic have, however, produced hints that long-term isolation can have adverse health effects. Long periods of isolation may impair the normal functioning of the

Isolation on Ice

Isolation is a fact of life not only for those scientists who remain over the winter at the Amundsen-Scott South Pole Station. Those who choose to endure Antarctica's harshest season at the two other United States scientific research stations in the Antarctic—McMurdo Station and Palmer Station—know what it is like to live in a place where connection with the outside world is difficult, if not altogether impossible.

McMurdo is located on Ross Island about 2,400 miles (3,840 kilometers) south of Christchurch, New Zealand. It was named for a nineteenth-century explorer, Lt. Archibald McMurdo, who visited the area. The United States chose the site because it is the world's most southern point of land that can regularly be reached by ship. McMurdo is the hub or center for the entire Antarctic Research Program. Into its harbor and ice runways come ships and planes carrying most scientists, equipment, fuel, food, and other supplies. Ski-equipped airplanes and helicopters ferry personnel and equipment from McMurdo to scientists working at other stations and small research camps.

In the busy summer research season, McMurdo looks much like a small town. During this October to January period of 24-hour sunlight, more than 1,200 people live and work in McMurdo. It has more than 100 permanent buildings. These include a hospital, fire station, library, church, weather station, living and eating quarters, a gym, bars, a power plant, repair shops, and a desalting plant to produce fresh water from the ocean.

During the winter period that extends from late February to August, McMurdo's population usually dips to 250 people. The station is isolated from the rest of the world during this time of 24-hour darkness. No planes land. No ships visit. Nobody enters, and nobody leaves. Scientists are isolated in a harsh climate. Winter temperatures have dipped to −58°F (−50°C). Strong winds often blow and intensify the cold.

Palmer Station was established in 1965 on the harbor of Anvers Island, about 600 miles (966 kilometers) south of Cape Horn at the tip of South America. It was named for Nathaniel B. Palmer, a Connecticut seal hunter who in 1820 was among the first humans to see the Antarctic.

The station consists of five buildings, two big fuel storage tanks, a dock, and other facilities. About fifty scientists and other personnel work there during the summer. Only about ten remain for the winter. People and supplies come to the station on two research ships, the R/V *Polar Duke* and the R/V *Nathaniel B. Palmer*. These ships can dock at Palmer during the winter, and the station is not as isolated as McMurdo or the South Pole. It also has a milder climate. The average annual temperature is 26°F (−3.33°C). Temperatures average 36°F (2.22°C) in December and 14°F (−10°C) in July.

The Polar Duke *at Palmer Station.*

body's immunological defense system, which protects against infections and other diseases. Unusual cycles of light and darkness like those in the Antarctic and on other planets are another source of concern. Human biorhythms, or biological clocks, run parallel to the 24-hour cycles of light and darkness on Earth. These internal clocks regulate appetite, sleep and wakefulness, mood, secretion of hormones, and other body functions. But normal day-night cycles disappear on other planets, as they do in the Antarctic.

ANTARCTIC TESTING GROUNDS

NASA plans to use two antarctic regions as living laboratories to prepare for other aspects of manned missions to the moon and Mars. One is an area around the South Pole known as the Polar Plateau. The plateau is a huge, desolate accumulation of ice, almost 2 miles (3 kilometers) thick in some spots. The air is so thin that people have difficulty breathing, and sometimes must use oxygen masks. The Polar Plateau would be used mainly to simulate artificial habitats, isolation, and other conditions encountered during long-duration space flights or long stays on planetary surfaces. Some of the research would be conducted at the existing South Pole station. But other locations on the plateau would provide better analogs of extraterrestrial sites. At some of these, the combination of high altitude and constant low atmospheric pressure produces environmental conditions equivalent to those found on top of a mountain 3 miles (5 kilometers) high. A Mars analog station built at such a site would—of necessity—be very realistic. It might, for instance, be fully pressurized, with the crew donning space suits to venture outside. Such a station would be ideal for testing the kinds of life-support system required on another planet. Energy supplies would come from solar power, wastes would be recycled in closed systems, and occupants might try to raise their own food.

Antarctica's dry valleys are the second site. The largest of these ice-free oases are located in southern Victoria Land near

Researchers at work in the dry valley region. This ice-free region provides a rare chance to sample the continent's rock and soil.

the Ross Sea. They consist of about 1,600 square miles (4,144 square kilometers) of barren, rock-strewn land. Unlike the rest of Antarctica, the dry valleys have no permanent ice or snow cover. They remain ice-free because the Transantarctic Mountains act as a barrier that prevent glaciers from flowing into the area from the Polar Plateau. The mountains stretch for 2,300 miles (3,680 kilometers), from the Ross Sea to the eastern edge of the Filchner Ice Shelf on the Weddell Sea. The valleys are the driest desert on Earth, with evaporation far exceeding annual snowfall.

Ice-covered lakes exist in the valleys, somewhat like the underground deposits of frozen water believed to exist on Mars. Indeed, the dry valleys have a climate similar to that on Mars. The average annual temperature in the antarctic valleys is about −4°F (−20°C). But temperatures can range from a wintertime low of −58°F (−50°C) to a summer high of 50°F (10°C). The sun shines constantly for about four months of the year, followed by two months of twilight, four months of total darkness, and two months of dawn. In the winter, powerful winds howl down from the Polar Plateau, eroding the landscape of the dry valleys like the winds on Mars.

EXOBIOLOGY: LIFE STRIVES TO ADAPT

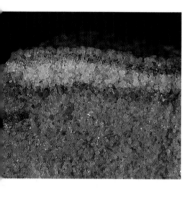

Variations in the color of this rock from the dry valleys signal the presence of cryptoendolithic organisms—microbes that survive antarctic conditions by living in rocks.

Ever since the Viking experiments, scientists have used the dry valleys for *exobiology*, geology, and other studies related to those planned for other planets. Exobiology is the study of forms of plant and animal life that might occur on other planets. This research would be intensified and expanded if NASA proceeds with plans for human exploration of Mars and other planets. Environmental conditions in the dry valleys have forced life to adapt to conditions resembling those on Mars. Microbes must survive in extreme cold, with very little water, under intense ultraviolet radiation from the sun. Soil in the Dry Valleys is extremely poor, with only small quantities of organic nutrients and minerals.

In a quest to survive, microorganisms actually have taken refuge inside rocks. These *cryptoendolithic organisms* live in the outer few millimeters of certain rocks in the dry valleys. Cryptoendolithic comes from words meaning "hidden" (crypto-), "inside" (endo-), and "rock" (lithic). Some scientists believe that Martian microbes were forced into the same kind of habitat during the last stages of extinction of life on the Red Planet. Studies of cryptoendolithic organisms are already helping scientists reconstruct events leading to the possible disappearance of life on Mars. In the future, they also may give researchers hints about what hidden forms of life might still survive on Mars today.

Biologists have discovered that other organisms make strange adaptations to survive in the unearthly dry valley environment. Among the survivors are nematodes, a family of small worms. Some nematodes live in thin films of water that surround soil particles. They play an important role in decomposing and recycling organic matter in the soil. Researchers have found nematodes living in a wide variety of soil conditions in the dry valleys. They undergo a strange transformation to survive during the very harshest conditions in Antarctica. Nematodes enter what almost seems like a state of suspended animation. Scientists call this a state of *cryptobiosis*, or hidden life. The nematodes have no detectable *metabolism*, the process by which all living things break down food to make energy. Yet the worms are capable of reviving and resuming life processes when warmer, more favorable environmental conditions return. Could cryptobiosis allow life to exist on Mars or other planets with inhospitable environments? Antarctic research could help supply the answer.

DUAL PURPOSE RESEARCH

Information from antarctic sites used as analogs for other planets may also prove to be useful here and now. A spellbinding example of this dual-purpose research took place in 1993 at the rim of Mount Erebus, an active volcano 12,477 feet (3,793 meters) high. Erebus is on Ross Island, within sight of the main United States base at McMurdo. The mountain was named for the passageway into hell of ancient Greek mythology. There the robot Dante performed experiments intended to test technology for robotic exploration of Mars and the moon.

Dante was built by Carnegie-Mellon University's Robotics

Clouds of steam and gas rise through the ice and snow around Mount Erebus, an active volcano near McMurdo Station, where conditions are among the harshest on Earth.

Institute in Pittsburgh. The project was sponsored by NASA and the National Science Foundation, which hope that an advanced version of Dante will roam Mars or the moon. Dante was named for Dante Alighieri, the Italian poet who lived from 1265 to 1321. *The Inferno,* part of his masterpiece, *The Divine Comedy,* described a journey into the mythical Erebus.

Robot engineers designed Dante to withstand harsh environmental conditions and to travel over rough terrain. It could step over boulders or other obstacles up to 4.8 feet (1.5 meters) high. Dante actually "felt" its way down the sides of ravines or craters by using laser range finders, 3-D video cameras, and eyelike proximity finders in its feet. The robot carried a variety of instruments to take temperature readings, measure the chemical composition of gases, and retrieve samples for later analysis.

Dante served as a prototype for future space robots. But it was also designed to measure the composition of Mount Erebus's volcanic gases. Scientists believe that Mount Erebus may produce large quantities of natural gases, including carbon dioxide, chlorine, and sulfur dioxide, that contribute to the antarctic ozone hole. Since scientists were unable to gather direct samples of the gases, they had to rely on measurements taken from a distance, after the gases were diluted by the atmosphere.

Dante's initial effort to crawl into the volcano's crater failed. But the failure helped increase scientific knowledge about the design of robots. More successful versions of Dante can now be built that may help scientists better understand the role natural gases play in ozone destruction.

Another dual-purpose technology being tested by NASA and the NSF in Antarctica is *telepresence*. Telepresence is an advanced form of remote control that gives a human operator control over the movements of a distant robot. Wearing a special video headset linked by computer to the robot, the operator can see through cameras on the robot as it operates in a place too dangerous or inaccessible for a human. The researcher can control movements of the robot's cameras by simply moving his or her head.

Antarctic scientists have made many tests of telepresence. In one project, for example, an aquatic "rover," a submersible robot vehicle, descended into Lake Hoare. Lake Hoare is a permanently ice-covered lake in the antarctic dry valleys. Using telepresence technology, the scientists controlled movements of the robot so that it could measure the lake's chemical, biological, and physical characteristics. The data permitted scientists to develop a three-dimensional profile of the lake's currents, dissolved oxygen, light levels, and distribution of microorganisms.

The research team established a field camp near the lake, just as future astronauts might do on Mars. Electricity for the robot experiments and other activities came from an advanced solar power system that can be deployed easily in remote places. Studies of the lake also may help scientists understand Mars's history, including how life may have vanished from the planet. The lake is believed to simulate conditions on Mars billions of years ago, when liquid water, so critical for life, still existed.

Experience with telepresence in the Antarctic will help in the development of similar technology for use in environments on Earth that are too hostile for humans. Using telepresence, for instance, engineers will be able to guide robots to take measurements and make repairs in highly radioactive areas of nuclear power plants. Rescue personnel hope to use telepresence in fires, mine disasters, and other kinds of accidents.

FIRE
AND ICE

One night Dr. Douglas Martinson, an oceanographer, was sound asleep in his tent on Ice Station Weddell. The temporary station was a cluster of thirty huts and tents on an ice floe. An ice floe is a sheet of ice that breaks off from the surrounding frozen ocean, and drifts in the currents and winds. The 1.7-mile (2.7-kilometer)-long sheet under the station was making its way through the least-explored body of water on Earth. Humans had not ventured into this mysterious region of the Antarctic's Weddell Sea for eighty years. Suddenly Dr. Martinson was awakened by the sound of heavy breathing that reminded him of the menacing breath of Darth Vader, arch-villain in the science-fiction thriller *Star Wars*. Then came another surprise. The tent filled with a horrible stink, like rotten fish. Dr. Martinson looked over toward a big hole drilled through the ice so that he could lower instruments into the frigid ocean and conduct experiments. Looking back at him, just as amazed, was a large, curious seal that had popped up for a breath of air while swimming beneath the 6-foot (2-meter)-thick ice.

Unexpected visitors were only one of the surprises for a hardy group of American and Russian scientists whose floating research site retraced the route of perhaps the greatest adventure in Antarctica's history. Ice Station Weddell drifted for four months through about 400 miles (644 kilometers) of the Weddell Sea, providing a base of operations for more than sixty

Ice meets water at the Weddell Sea. In 1992, a research station on the ice allowed scientists to conduct extensive studies of this little-known region.

scientists, while following the path of Sir Ernest Shackleton's ship, *Endurance*. In 1915, *Endurance* became frozen, or beset, in the ice and drifted for more than nine months before being crushed. Shackleton's aim was adventure. The great British explorer was attempting to land a crew that would be the first to cross the Antarctic continent.

Dr. Martinson and his crew of modern-day explorers had a much different goal. They were making some of the very first measurements of an important part of the Weddell Sea. Unlike the rest of the Weddell, this western region is perpetually covered with ice and has never been studied by research ships. Some of the few existing measurements, in fact, were made by Shackleton's crew. Except for other reports from ships that were also beset in the ice, and from satellite images, scientists knew little about the region. Now Ice Station Weddell's crew was finally making sensitive measurements of the interactions between ocean, ice, and atmosphere in this region.

PROBING THE WEDDELL SEA

Ice Station Weddell was set up in February 1992 by American and Russian scientists. They sailed into the Weddell Sea on the Russian icebreaker and research vessel *Akademik Fedorov*, which unloaded more than 80 tons of supplies and equipment onto a floe chosen for the station. Bulldozers and helicopters distributed the cargo carefully to avoid overloading and cracking the ice. Bulldozers also carved out an ice runway so that small ski-equipped planes could land, and moved into position the preassembled huts and tents scientists would live in. The station included a mess hall, storehouses, generators, latrines, and even a sauna that was used once a week. Drinking water came from melted snow. Up to thirty-seven scientists lived at the station at a time. Helicopters ferried crews of men and women in and out during the 117-day mission. A total of sixty scientists spent time on the floe. They included oceanographers, biologists, and other specialists. Each had 72 pounds (33 kilograms) of cold-weather clothing. Temperatures ranged from 29°F to −33°F (−1.7°C to −36°C), with the wind chill sometimes dipping to −60°F (−51°C).

At one point, the ice floe suddenly split, creating an open channel of water that divided the camp in half. It also destroyed the ice runway. After that, supplies arrived by parachute or helicopter. The incident prompted scientists to keep boats nearby for an evacuation in case of further cracks.

Scientists and divers had access to the ocean through large holes bored in the ice. Each hole was enclosed in a heated hut to prevent it from freezing over. As the floe drifted, scientists conducted research to determine the Weddell Sea's role in global ocean circulation and climate.

ANTARCTICA'S CLIMATE MACHINE

The Weddell Sea is only about as big as the Gulf of Mexico, and so obscure that it doesn't even appear on many maps. But scientists believe it is of global importance. The Weddell Sea belongs to the southern ocean surrounding Antarctica. Formed by the Atlantic, Pacific, and Indian oceans, the southern ocean interacts with the atmosphere around Antarctica. The ocean and atmosphere exchange energy, water, and gas in ways that determine the temperature, chemical composition, and motion of the oceans and atmosphere throughout the rest of the world.

Flowing northward out of the Antarctic is an immense current of frigid water. It flows at a rate of 130 million cubic feet (3.6 million cubic meters) per *second*.[1] In contrast, the flow of the Amazon, the Nile, the Mississippi, and all the world's other rivers *combined* is only about 1 million cubic feet (28,000 cubic meters) per second.[2] The current, which originates in the Weddell Sea, plays a key role in the processes that keep Europe warm, make America's Pacific Northwest so wet and cloudy, and the western coast of South America dry.

This occurs as the result of a process in which deep ocean currents circulate continuously between the Antarctic and northern parts of the world in a kind of loop.

In the tropical and subtropical regions of the planet, heat from the sun penetrates below the water's surface, warming the deeper ocean waters. Sunlight also evaporates water at the surface, concentrating the surface water's salt. The excess salt also spreads, or diffuses, downward. The result is a mass of warm, salty water that flows southward into the southern ocean, where it rises or "upwells."

On the surface, this water releases huge quantities of heat, then cools. It also becomes less salty by mixing with fresh water from melted ice and snow. In the western Weddell Sea, this water becomes very cold and dense and sinks toward the ocean bottom. The bottom water spreads northward along the sea floor, beyond the equator. This water is responsible for maintaining the cold temperatures of deep ocean waters around the world. As the water travels north, it gradually mixes with warmer, more salty water from the surface, and the circulation cycle begins anew. The circulation helps to determine how much global temperatures vary with latitude from north to south. This variation affects many of the processes that determine Earth's climate and local weather conditions.

The overturning, rising, and sinking in the southern ocean also have an effect much like opening a window on the ocean. These processes actually "ventilate" deep ocean waters. They cool the water, lower the salt content, or salinity, and replenish oxygen used up by marine animals.

A CARBON DIOXIDE SINK

In the southern ocean, these interactions between warmer and colder waters may also have an important impact in determining the seriousness of the greenhouse effect. The greenhouse effect is one of our major global environmental concerns. It occurs when certain *greenhouse gases*, particularly *carbon dioxide*, are released by industrial and agricultural activity and accumulate in the atmosphere. Carbon dioxide in the atmosphere acts like the panes of glass in a greenhouse. It allows heat rays from the sun to enter the atmosphere. But it then prevents some of the heat from escaping back to space. As carbon dioxide accumulates, more heat is trapped and the Earth warms. Higher global temperatures could have adverse effects, making some of our richest agricultural land unsuitable for farming, or melting the polar ice caps, raising ocean levels, and flooding coastal cities.

Scientists believe that the southern ocean may be a major "sink" for carbon dioxide. Throughout the world, there is a constant interchange, or flux, of carbon dioxide between air and water. There is a certain concentration of carbon dioxide in the air and a certain concentration in the water. The air contains about 700 billion tons of carbon dioxide.[3] The oceans contain more than 35,000 billion tons of carbon dioxide.[4] Carbon dioxide moves back and forth between oceans and atmosphere to maintain those levels.

But the southern ocean seems to absorb more carbon dioxide than it releases. Phytoplankton in the southern ocean "lock up" the carbon dioxide. They use the carbon dioxide to make nutrients and energy during photosynthesis. As a result, the southern ocean's phytoplankton may slow global warming from the greenhouse effect.

What effect will greenhouse warming have on the interactions between ice, ocean, and air that make the southern ocean a carbon dioxide sink? Could global warming alter ice conditions, and in doing so cause sudden, dramatic shifts in climate? What effect could the greenhouse effect have on the antarctic ice cap? Are warmer global temperatures really the trigger that caused the collapse of ice sheets in the past?

A scientist at the Weddell Ice Station draws water samples from the edge of the ice.

(75)

Such questions lure scientists like Dr. Martinson to the Weddell Ice Station. Searching for answers involves many techniques.

In one of the huts, for instance, scientists lowered a cable deep into the water every 10 to 15 miles (16 to 24 kilometers). Attached to the cable were water-collection bottles designed to take water samples from different depths of the ocean. The samples were analyzed for dissolved gases, nutrients, and other materials. Scientists learned about circulation patterns with tests that showed whether the water came from the Pacific or Atlantic oceans. They studied the exchange of heat and gases between the atmosphere, the ice, and the ocean; the circulation of heat and salt in water below the ice; water temperatures; and other topics.

The mission drew to a close on June 5, 1992, when scientists began loading their gear on the *Akademik Fedorov* and the brand-new American icebreaker and research vessel *Nathaniel B. Palmer*. They removed everything, including unused fuel, to avoid polluting the ocean when the floe finally melted.

Among their initial discoveries, scientists found that the continental slope off the Antarctic Peninsula is about 62 miles (100 kilometers) farther west than was previously thought.[5] The continental slope is the region just beyond the continental shelf, the relatively shallow part of the sea floor bordering most continents. The continental slope descends steeply into the sea bed in the open ocean. This major discovery will change scientific understanding of ocean circulation patterns. Ice Station Weddell scientists also found new clues that may help explain why the western Weddell Sea remains covered with thick ice all year, unlike the eastern Weddell where ice melts in the summer and remains thin in winter.

Scientists will need years to fully analyze data from Ice Station Weddell to better understand the critical air-sea-ice interactions in the Weddell Sea. Their studies may fill major gaps in knowledge that now limit our understanding of the greenhouse effect. Scientists try to predict the severity and consequences of greenhouse warming with computer "models." These sets of mathematical equations simulate the effects of increased amounts of carbon dioxide in the atmosphere under various conditions. Data from the Weddell project may provide a valuable supplement to these models of our environment's future.

ICE IN MOTION

Far across the Weddell Sea, ice of another kind may also reveal secrets about Earth's future and prehistoric past. It is the vast continental ice sheet that covers almost the entire surface of Antarctica. In most places the ice is just over a mile thick, but it sometimes reaches a depth of 3 miles (5 kilometers).[6] Scientists estimate that if this ice melted, it would raise the world's ocean levels by more than 180 feet (55 meters).[7] The ice, which accumulated over millions of years, is so heavy that it actually has compressed the underlying rock. Although the ice may look solid and immovable, it does not stay still. It flows steadily into the sea, where it breaks apart or "calves" into huge chunks. These icebergs may float hundreds of miles before melting and adding their water to the sea. Much of the ice is carried into the sea in mighty ice streams. These are faster-moving areas of ice that flow through glaciers.

Scientists once thought that the antarctic ice cap was permanent. They believed that it formed about 14 million years ago and remained stable except for minor variations in size. But studies of glaciers and ice cores have challenged this idea. Ice cores are cylinders of ice that scientists can obtain from thousands of feet below the surface. Ice in the cores was deposited hundreds of thousands of years ago. Gases, dust, and other material trapped in the ice provide a frozen record of environmental conditions that existed in the distant past.

Icebergs—huge floating chunks of sea ice—drift across the Weddell Sea.

A scientist examines a core from the antarctic ice cap. Such samples reveal the history of environmental changes over thousands of years.

In cores taken from deep inside the West Antarctic Ice Sheet (WAIS), a part of the south polar ice cap that covers a big area of the continent, scientists have detected the fossilized remains of sea-dwelling algae. They concluded that open ocean existed in this interior portion of Antarctica about 2 million years ago.[8] Thus the ice sheet, far from being permanent, must have collapsed in the past and began re-forming less than 2 million years ago. Scientists have other evidence that the ice sheet melted and re-formed many times in the past. The melting may have occurred in a relatively sudden and unpredictable fashion.

Some of the evidence suggests that melting occurred because ice streams began to flow very rapidly, draining so much ice from the WAIS that the entire sheet collapsed. Scientists thus are particularly interested in identifying factors that could cause the rapid flow of ice streams.

The Nathaniel B. Palmer *at the Weddell Ice Station.*

Science Afloat

At 3:00 A.M. I awaken terrified by the clanging noise and powerful vibrations cascading through the R/V *Nathaniel B. Palmer,* an ice breaker and oceanographic research vessel that will be my home for three weeks. This is my third trip to the frozen continent. But never have I heard or felt anything like this.

Imagine sitting inside a metal pipe while people beat the sides with heavy steel chains and baseball bats. The huge ship, which is longer than a football field and towers five stories above the water, vibrates so strongly that it seems as if we've run aground and are steaming over rough land. The din makes conversation impossible. But a trip to the bridge brings reassurance from Captain Joseph Borkowski that all is well. The *Natty B.,* as the ship is fondly called by scientists, is simply doing its job: noisily crunching through pack ice 3 feet (1 meter) thick while carrying geologists on an expedition in the Ross Sea.

The *Palmer* and its research team are continuing the oldest tradition of research in the frozen continent. The very earliest scientific studies of the antarctic region were simple measurements of wind speed, ocean temperature, currents, and depth made from sailing vessels, often ships that were in the area to hunt whales or seals.

Some of today's most sophisticated antarctic research still is done from ships. But they are research vessels that sail only for science, and are outfitted as floating scientific laboratories. The *Nathaniel B. Palmer*, which first sailed in 1992 to bring personnel and supplies to Ice Station Weddell, is the newest and most advanced. Much of the *Palmer's* research is done in ice-bound areas of the southern ocean that cannot be reached by other vessels. The ship has eight laboratories, and a wide variety of instruments for research in biology, geology, oceanography, and other fields. Helicopters can land on the deck, and ferry personnel and equipment to remote research sites.

Teams of thirty-seven scientists, plus a crew of twenty-six, can stay at sea on the *Palmer* for as long as seventy-five days. They berth in comfortable cabins that have private bathrooms, television, and VCR; exercise in a small gym; and relax in a sauna. Every minute on the ship is precious, and scientists usually work in shifts twenty-four hours a day to gather as much data as possible. It costs the National Science Foundation $40,000 a *day* to operate the *Palmer*.

As I quickly learned, ice breakers do much of their heaviest work not by crashing head-on into the ice but by riding up onto it, by "backing and ramming." The front hull, made from steel several inches thick, slides up onto a sheet of ice so the ship's weight can fracture the ice. The ship then backs off and repeats the process. Like other ice breakers, the *Palmer* has a special feature to keep it from becoming stuck in the ice, as was Shackleton's *Endurance*. Special water tanks on each side can be alternately flooded and emptied to rock the vessel from side to side until it works free.

America's other floating laboratory is the R/V *Polar Duke*, a 219-foot (67-meter) vessel launched in 1983. The *Duke* has a special strengthened hull that withstands pressure from ice, but it is not an ice breaker. The ship carries teams of twenty-seven scientists, plus a crew of fourteen, on voyages around the Antarctic Peninsula.

One of the most fascinating theories suggests that volcanic eruptions occurring underneath the West Antarctic Ice Sheet may cause its sudden collapse. Scientists believe that heat from the volcanoes is not the direct cause. Rather, they suspect that this heat produces water that mixes with soil to lubricate the surface of the earth beneath the ice sheet. By creating this slippery film, the water causes the ice sheet to move more quickly into the sea. Any increase in volcanic activity thus could propel the ice sheet toward melting in the ocean.

Scientists have evidence that such volcanoes do exist.[9] They have flown over the ice in airplanes rigged with radar and other sensing devices. The sensors can determine the thickness of the ice, and the nature of the rock formations underneath it. The data show the characteristic "signature" of volcanic rock. In addition, the location of these volcanic formations coincides with circular depressions on the ice surface that have been detected from airplane and satellite images. The depressions do not move with the ice sheet, and also suggest the presence of underground volcanoes that produce heat and cause melting at the base of the ice sheet.

The information is important because melting of the WAIS would raise ocean levels by about 18 feet (5.5 meters), flooding coastal areas where most of the world's people live.[10] Some scientists believe that an increase in the flow of ice streams could cause sea levels to rise quickly, within 100 to 200 years.[11] Advance warning from Antarctica's ice in motion could give the world time to prepare for the flood.

CONCLUSION

Scientific research in Antarctica began as part of the adventure of exploring the frozen continent. But even when the International Geophysical Year began in 1957, research remained only one of many motives for being in Antarctica. Many countries competed with one another for political influence in the world as part of the Cold War, and used antarctic bases as symbols of influence and expansion. When the Cold War ended in the early 1990s, it left Antarctica free at last to fully live up to its name as a continent for science.

Even with all the work being done on the continent opposite the bear, scientific exploration in Antarctica has only just begun. What wonders will explorers in this global Age of Science discover about Earth and the universe, our distant past and our future?

NOTES

CHAPTER ONE

1. Ron Scherer, "Plumbing the Southern Ocean," *Christian Science Monitor*, August 10, 1991.
2. William Booth, "America and Antarctica: Long Separated Siblings," *The Washington Post*, March 27, 1991.
3. "Antarctica," *The World Book Encyclopedia*, Vol. 1, 1987, p. 530.
4. *The United States Antarctic Program* (Washington, D. C.: National Science Foundation, 1990), p. 10.
5. Ibid.
6. Ibid.
7. Ibid, p. 29.

CHAPTER TWO

1. Christopher Anderson, "Penguins Losing the Struggle?" *Nature*, Vol. 350, March 28, 1991, p. 294.
2. Ibid.

CHAPTER THREE

1. Owen B. Toon and Richard P. Turco, "Polar Stratospheric Clouds and Ozone Depletion," *Scientific American*, June 1991, p. 8.
2. "Air," *The World Book Encyclopedia*, Vol. 1, 1987, p. 157.
3. Ibid., p. 160.

4. Ibid., p. 157.

5. John Noble Wilford, "Antarctic Ozone Hole Hits Record Low," *The New York Times*, October 19, 1993.

6. Ibid.

7. Cheryl Dybas, "Antarctic Food Chain Decreasing in Response to Ultraviolet-Light-Induced Damage," National Science Foundation News Release, February 20, 1992.

8. Tim Tomastik, "Ozone Layer Thins Over U.S.," National Oceanic and Atmospheric Administration News Release, September 23, 1993.

9. *Production, Sales, and Calculated Release of CFC-11 and CFC-12 Through 1987* (Washington, D. C.: Chemical Manufacturers Association, 1988).

10. Richard S. Stolarski, "The Antarctic Ozone Hole," *Scientific American*, January 1988, p. 30.

11. "Ozone Depletion," *CO Researcher*, Vol. 2, April 3, 1992, p. 299.

CHAPTER FOUR

1. William A. Cassidy, "Antarctic Search for Meteorites (ANSMET)," *United States Antarctic Program 1993-94 Science Program Plan* (Washington, D. C.: National Science Foundation), p. S-64.

CHAPTER FIVE

1. Interview with Dr. Matthew Houseal, Amundsen-Scott South Pole Station, November 13, 1991.

CHAPTER SIX

1. Scherer, p. 10.

2. Ibid.

3. Lecture by Dr. Arnold Gordon, professor of oceanography, Lamont-Doherty Geophysical Observatory, Columbia University, presented September 14, 1992, at the National Science Foundation Antarctic Orientation Seminar, Washington, D. C.

4. Ibid.

5. Cheryl Dybas, "Scientists Report on Research Findings in Previously Unexplored Antarctic Sea," National Science Foundation News Release, December 4, 1992.

6. *The United States Antarctic Program* (Washington, D. C.: National Science Foundation, 1990), p. 10.

7. Ibid.

8. Richard Monastersky, "When Antarctica Melted Away," *Science News,* February 13, 1993, p. 107.

9. Ibid.

10. Ibid.

11. Donald D. Blankenship, "Active Volcanism Beneath the West Antarctic Ice Sheet and Implications for Ice-Sheet Stability," *Nature,* Vol. 361, February 11, 1993, p. 526.

GLOSSARY

Anisotropy. Variations in a substance that otherwise is uniform.

Atmosphere. The blanket of oxygen, nitrogen, carbon dioxide, water vapor, and other gases that surrounds Earth. From bottom to top, it consists of the troposphere, stratosphere, mesosphere, and thermosphere.

Big Bang theory. The theory that the universe formed 15 to 20 billion years ago in a massive explosion that created stars, galaxies, and other matter.

Black holes. The remnants of collapsed stars so dense that light cannot escape.

Carbon dioxide. A gas produced in the combustion of fuels and burning of tropical rain forests that is the biggest cause of the greenhouse effect.

Chlorofluorocarbons. Industrial chemicals, also known as CFCs, that destroy atmospheric ozone. CFCs are being replaced by environmentally safer chemicals.

Cosmic rays. Radiation coming from space that consists mainly of high-energy subatomic particles called protons and electrons.

Cryptobiosis. A state in which organisms survive harsh environmental conditions by slowing down their metabolism. They appear dead, yet can revive when favorable conditions return.

Cryptoendolithic organisms. Microbes that survive harsh environmental conditions by living inside the pores of rock.

Ecosystem. A community that consists of all the living and nonliving things that interact in a given area of space, such as an ocean or forest, to form a stable system.

Electromagnetic spectrum. All the different forms of radiation, including visible light, radio waves, microwaves, X rays, ultraviolet, and infrared.

Exobiology. The study of unusual forms of plant and animal life similar to those that could exist on other planets.

Food chain. A group of organisms that depend on one another for food, transferring energy from its primary source in plants to animals that eat plants and each other.

Food web. Several different food chains that overlap or interlock.

Greenhouse effect. A warming of Earth's climate that occurs when certain gases in the atmosphere block release of heat energy into space, much like the panes of glass in a greenhouse.

Greenhouse gases. Carbon dioxide, methane, and other gases that accumulate in Earth's atmosphere and contribute to global warming.

Infrared light. Radiation that lies beyond red in the spectrum and cannot be seen because its wavelength is longer than visible light. It can be felt as heat.

Krill. Small shrimplike animals found in enormous numbers in the ocean around Antarctica.

Metabolism. The chemical changes in living cells that provide energy for all the life functions of plants and animals.

Meteorite. A piece of stone or metal from space that plunges through the atmosphere and lands on Earth's surface.

Molecule. A group of atoms chemically bonded together.

Neutrinos. Hard-to-detect atomic particles, produced in nuclear reactions in celestial bodies, which penetrate all matter yet leave little trace as they pass through.

Neutron stars. Extremely dense objects that remain when stars explode.

Ozone. A form of the gas oxygen (O_2) that contain three oxygen atoms (O_3).

Ozone hole. An area of the atmosphere over Anarctica where ozone levels decline in the spring, allowing excess ultraviolet light to reach Earth's surface.

Ozone layer. A region of the stratosphere where ordinary oxygen (O_2) breaks down and reforms into ozone, which shields Earth from harmful ultraviolet radiation.

Photosynthesis. The process in which plants use sunlight, carbon dioxide, and water to make nutrients and oxygen.

Phytoplankton. Small drifting aquatic plants, such as algae, that use photosynthesis to produce their own food and are the ultimate food source for all antarctic animals.

Stratosphere. The layer of the atmosphere that extends from about 10 to 30 miles (16 to 48 kilometers) above Earth's surface and includes the ozone layer.

Telepresence. Remote-control technology that allows humans to direct movement of robots from a distance.

Troposphere. The layer of atmosphere closest to the earth.

Ultraviolet light. Radiation that lies beyond violet in the spectrum and cannot be seen because its wavelength is shorter than visible light. Excessive exposure can cause skin cancer and other health problems.

FOR FURTHER INFORMATION

Note: Before ordering any materials or using any services, be sure to find out if a fee will be charged.

GENERAL INFORMATION

The National Science Foundation Office of Polar Programs has pamphlets, reports, and other information concerning Antarctica and the U.S. Antarctic Research Program. Write: Polar Information Program, Office of Polar Programs, National Science Foundation, 4201 Wilson Blvd., Arlington, Va. 22230.

The Library of Congress maintains a comprehensive bibliography of virtually all literature about Antarctica published worldwide since 1951. Called the *Antarctic Bibliography*, it includes titles, abstracts, and indexes. The subject categories are: general, biological sciences, cartography, expeditions, geological sciences, ice and snow, logistics equipment and supplies, medical sciences, meteorology, oceanography, atmospheric physics, terrestrial physics, and political geography. Many of the listings are results of antarctic research that has been published in scientific journals. The Library of Congress also issues monthly abstracts of new antarctic literature. For a flyer write the NSF Polar Information Program.

A bibliography of earlier scientific, technical, and popular literature about the Antarctic was prepared by the U.S. Navy in 1951. It includes literature published from the earliest times to 1951. This *Antarctic Bibliography* has been reprinted by the Greenwood Press, 51 Riverside Avenue, Westport, Connecticut 06880.

If you have a computer with a modem, you can gain electronic access to antarctic information through NSF's Science and Technology Information Service (STIS). Call 703-306-1130 and request the "STIS Flyer," NSF Publication #91-10. Requests also can be made with an E-mail message. The address on Internet is *stisinfo@nsf.gov* and on Bitnet is *stisinfo@nsf.*

MAPS

The U.S. Geological Survey sells maps of different parts of Antarctica. An index and order forms are available free from: Distribution Branch, U.S. Geological Survey, Box 25286, Federal Center, Bldg. 41, Denver, Colorado 80225. Ask for the "Index to Topographical Maps Antarctica."

The Scientific Committee on Antarctic Research (SCAR) has many aerial photographs, maps, and satellite images produced by the United States and other countries. For a list write: Earth Science Information Center, U.S. Geological Survey, 507 USGS National Center, Reston, Virginia 22092.

The *Gazetteer of the Antarctic* lists more than 12,000 officially recognized place names of mountains, bays, and other geographical features, plus their geographic coordinates. Write to the NSF Polar Information Program.

BOOKS

Bertrand, Kenneth J. *Americans in Antarctica.* New York: American Geographical Society, 1971.

Hackwell, W. John. *Desert of Ice: Life & Work in Antarctica.* New York: Macmillan, 1991.

Land, Barbara. *The New Explorers: Women in Antarctica.* New York: Dodd, Mead, 1981.

Lansing, Alfred. *Endurance: Shackleton's Incredible Voyage.* New York: McGraw-Hill, 1959.

Neider, Charles, ed. *Antarctica: Authentic Accounts of Life and Exploration.* New York: Random House, 1972.

Reader's Digest Editors. *Antarctica: Great Stories from the Frozen Continent.* New York: Reader's Digest Services, 1985.

Shapley, Deborah. *The Seventh Continent: Antarctica in a Resource Age.* Washington, D.C.: Resources for the Future, 1986.

Sullivan, Walter. *Quest for a Continent.* New York: McGraw-Hill, 1957.

MAGAZINE ARTICLES

Andersen, Per H. "Astrophysics Goes South." *Science,* June 14, 1991, p. 1494.

Gordon, Arnold L., and Josefino C. Comiso. "Polynyas in the Southern Ocean." *Scientific American,* June 1988, p. 90.

Harvey, J., M. Pomerantz, and T. Duval. "Astronomy on Ice." *Sky & Telescope,* December 1982, p. 89.

Hodgson, Bryan. "Antarctica: A Land of Isolation No More." *National Geographic,* April 1990, p. 2.

Monastersky, Richard. "Fire Beneath the Ice." *Science News,* February 13, 1993, p. 101.

Monastersky, Richard. "The Cold Facts of Life." *Science News,* April 24, 1993, p. 135.

Parfit, Michael. "The Last Continent." *Smithsonian,* October 1984.

Parfit, Michael. "Nations Are Debating the Future of the Antarctic's Frozen Assets." *Smithsonian,* November 1984.

Radok, Uwe. "The Antarctic Ice." *Scientific American,* August 1985, p. 98.

Smith, David H. "Cosmic Fire, Terrestrial Ice." *Sky & Telescope,* November 1989, p. 192.

Sullivan, Walter. "Adrift at the Bottom of the World." *The New York Times Magazine,* November 1, 1992, p. 35.

INDEX